BETTER F*CKING GOLF

How I Went from Hacker to Club Champ Without Changing My Swing or Expensive Lessons

Paul Nardozzi

Acknowledgements

To my wife Laura: Thank you for being so patient and understanding of my passion for golf. With 3 small children, you are a saint for allowing me to spend hours away from home to play the game I love. This book wouldn't be possible without your love and support.

Contents

Chapter 1: The F*cking Intro

All right, well, I got you to buy my book. It's probably because of the f*cking title, but hey, how else is an amateur golfer going to sell golf books? What I've noticed over the years is that learning golf from golf professionals is not realistic. They're so deep into their own learning curve, that they've forgotten what it was like when they first started off. Mostly, because they were so young when they learned the game. They take for granted what feels natural for them and for us hackers, feels completely unnatural. It's kind of like your attractive and funny friend trying to relate to you about how hard it is to pick up girls at the bar. They're trying their best, but the reality is they have no f*cking clue what it's really like to be ugly and boring like friends of mine (definitely not me). This book will really add value to your golf game because I went through the transition of hacker to scratch entirely in my adult years. I have a clear understanding of what the average golfer is thinking and feeling. Golf professionals honestly can't relate and therefore the instruction you get from them isn't nearly as helpful.

I'm going to start this book off with two words that will validate everything I'm about to tell you: *Jim Furyk*. All right, well, that's sort of a joke—but not really, and here's why. From one of the top personalities in golf today, David Feherty describes Furyk's swing as "It looks like an octopus falling out of a tree." Feherty's humor adds a great twist to the game of golf; but aside from this assessment being hilarious, it's seriously thought-provoking. Jim is the epitome of throwing traditional swing mechanics out of the window and utilizing what feels comfortable and reproducible.

I eventually got to this point while watching the golf channel for endless hours and YouTube swing videos until I couldn't keep my f*cking eyes open. If you're reading this book, I bet you've been there before too. But in all seriousness, if Jim can take a swing out of a Dr. Seuss book and win major championships, why in the hell can't I take my current swing and become just a scratch golfer? That's when I started to research and experiment with things outside of the actual swing to make my game more consistent. I wasn't looking to make it on tour—well, maybe it was a shitty pipe dream—but there had to be something more to this. It can't be that only people with perfect swing mechanics can play good f*cking golf.

I started to look at other so-called no-name tour pros' swings on YouTube. I slowly began to realize that everyone has a different swing and different style yet produced similar outcomes in the actual shot. I then focused my efforts on understanding what they all did that was the same. If they didn't all swing the same, then what were they doing that *was* the same? Ultimately, I concluded that there are 5 essential aspects of the game that all the pros do exceptionally well; aim and proper alignment, head stability, follow through, swing tempo, and descending ball contact. After years of trial and error, I finally narrowed down some techniques that consistently help replicate those 5 things.

First though, let's talk about the shit you definitely will not read about in this book. My least favorite golf advice that we have all heard at least once: change your grip. Let's be honest for a second—have you ever actually tried changing your f*cking grip? I mean, if you're looking to spend a lot of time and money on a Sunday morning in misery and mother effing yourself, go for a grip change. Wouldn't it just be easier to finally get around to building that patio furniture your wife has been nagging you about for months? These lessons are easier than changing your swing mechanics, too. I bet there's been a time (or hundreds of times, in my case) where you've tried a new move on the range, and you think you've got it all figured out. When it's time to hit the course, you give up on it after the 3rd hole. I did all the embarrassing and frustrating chunking, so you don't have to. Fifteen f*cking years of it to be exact.

Before you get your panties in a bunch when I say it took me fifteen years, just know that it took me that long for a couple of reasons. For starters, when I first started, I was broke as shit. Spending thousands on swing lessons was not a thing for me. Then throw in a wife and three small kids in the second half of those 15 years and it didn't leave me with much time to play (also broke again). So, the only option for me was to figure it out on my own and that meant a shit ton of experimenting. Hell, I even played an entire season swinging with one arm. That's how committed I was to finding ways to play better golf. Lucky for you, I decided to put myself out there and write this book. Hopefully, I can spare someone else their sanity on the course. You're f*cking welcome.

Oh, and by the way, for all you English majors out there. I will give you a preemptive, f*ck off. I know I'm a shitty writer, let's just try to focus on the content and not the delivery, cool?

* * *

In full transparency, this book will not likely propel you to a PGA tour type of game, but it will help you reproducibly return the club to the same position you start your swing. If you ask me, that's really the name of the game; whatever happens from when you take the club away until contact doesn't really matter. We will accomplish this without all the confusing and complicated swing instruction you would get from a teaching professional or a golf magazine.

Trying to replicate the swing of a touring pro is a recipe for disaster. Trust me, I've tried it, and lost a few golf seasons trying to look like Tiger Woods on the course. This is usually what every golf magazine is selling you as well. *Look at what "insert everyone's favorite f*cking PGA tour golfer of the month" is doing and this is how he does it. Let's not f*cking mention he's been training all day, every day since he was seven, but hey weekend golfer, buy a subscription from us and you can have a swing just like his!* If you aren't a single-digit handicap already, and honestly, even if you are, it likely will lead to frustration and you reverting to your old swing pretty f*cking quickly.

Early on I took three lessons and that was all I needed to understand what the hell was actually happening. Swing coaches want to keep you coming back week after week. Look, I get it—they're trying to put food on the table just like the rest of us. So, what do they do? They focus on adjusting your grip and changing the way you pull back your club. And why do they focus on these two things? Because it feels uncomfortable, and it takes many lessons before you start to even develop a feel for it. If you're one of the lucky 5% to get past these two major fixes, then it's on to the downswing, which will likely keep you in the f*cking rabbit hole for months. My grip sucks and my swing sure as hell ain't pretty, but I found a way to become a scratch golfer and I think I have some ways to help other people do that too.

I could go on and on about golf instructors and their tactics to keep customers coming back, but that would probably require a whole other book. I will say that there are plenty of good instructors out there that actually want to help you get better. They tend to be at private country clubs, and they charge rates way out of my comfort zone and out of the comfort zone of a large majority of golfers. The teaching pro at my current golf club is one of the best in the business. He is outstanding at what he does and is someone I really respect. Hey, if you can afford it, this route might work for you. But for most of us, we just want to play better f*cking golf and not be frustrated the entire time we are on the course.

The following statement is the basis for my entire golf game and everything in this book: **Variability causes inconsistent results. Reducing the variables in your approach and swing increases consistency, and therefore success.** That's a f*cking loaded statement, I get it, so let's break that down. By definition, *variability* is the lack of a fixed pattern, or a liability to vary or change. We are essentially focusing on specific actions within the golf swing and approach that change from swing to swing.

For example, someone may line up to the right of the target on one swing, and the left of the target on the next. With two identical swings, you will produce two entirely different shots. Another example is someone who moves their head backward during the backswing. On one swing, they return their head to the starting position correctly, and on another swing, they can't, and it lags behind. Again, assuming the same swing, these will produce two entirely different shots.

The actual golf swing is probably the hardest thing to change and control. That's why a majority of PGA Tour pros have been getting swing instruction since they learned to walk and continuously need to fine tune their swing weekly. That's why this book focuses on the more important things within the approach to essentially make the actual swing irrelevant (thanks, Furyk). If we can control everything else, and therefore reduce the number of variables in our swing from, say, six things to one thing, you will see massive improvement. I will share with you the most common variables in an amateur golfer's game, along with the ones I dealt with myself and how to ultimately remove those variables. Hopefully, the lessons I have learned over the past 15 years can translate into your game a lot f*cking faster than it did for me.

Chapter2: My F*cking Background

It's probably best for me to give you a quick introduction about myself and my journey in golf to give you a better grasp of who I am, my skill level, and background. Growing up, I played golf casually with buddies. I took it way too seriously because I was so competitive, but I had a baseball swing of all baseball swings. I played a 60-yard slice like it was my f*cking job—well, sometimes. Okay, okay, just about never, but that one time per round that I did, it was f*cking awesome.

I was a baseball player by trade. I was recruited by a lot of D1 schools and received a full scholarship to pitch for the University of Pittsburgh. I broke a 50-year-old career strikeout record there, and it propelled me to get drafted by the Detroit Tigers. By the time I was in pro ball, I had a lot of shoulder issues and eventually tore a ligament that knocked me out of the game.

Now, before any of you start the whole "He was a professional athlete, and he did this and did that, and I was never good at sports," rigmarole, just remember that I was a pitcher, not a hitter, so I was never good at the swing part of it. But I will say that there are a lot of similarities you can draw from the pitching delivery and the golf swing. It's a quick motion that requires multiple body parts to work in harmony to deliver a result which is not affected by any external variables. Yeah, I know, I tend to nerd out from time to time, so just bear with me. What I mean by that is, unlike a jump shot in basketball, where a defender can be in your face and force you to change your mechanics, or a quarterback in football with a defensive end coming in hot, forcing him to throw on the run, golf has no external factors. Aside from that oak tree your ball is sitting up against, or someone yelling "FORE" in your backswing, the golf swing can be rehearsed and is premeditated every time.

I started to take golf seriously once I was done with baseball. I needed something to distract me from the fact that I had spent my entire life chasing after a dream I had since I was a kid, and now it was all over. So, I drowned myself in golf instead of booze to distract myself from the harsh reality of a lifelong dream now over. All right, fine. I hit the booze pretty hard too, but golf was ultimately my savior. Now the better I get, the more I love the game.

I started at a low-cost country club that was affordable, and where I knew there were good players I could learn from. The first thing I did was ask the head pro when the scratch players played. I made it a point to hang out with them and hopefully learn a lesson or two from them. The first lesson being, don't ask for strokes, and the most important lesson, bring a lot of money to the course "just in case".

The first couple of years at the club cost me more money on the course than the dues I paid monthly, but what I learned from that group of golfers was invaluable for my game. I went from a 16 handicap to a 10 handicap pretty quickly. I spent the following four years at another club getting a feel for my game, and really started to work on my short game. Once I figured out how to get up and down from around the green, I got my handicap down to a 7. At this point, I was still a very inconsistent golfer. I could post a 73 or an 88 on any given day, and with GHIN only taking the average of your top 10 scores out of your last 20, that made for a very frustrating situation when making golf bets. I was either the guy that was full of shit about how good he was at golf, or the biggest f*cking sandbagger there was. Either way, it wasn't a good situation to be in, and I knew I had to get more consistent.

Having that big of a swing from my best to my worst rounds, I knew consistency was the only way I could get into that club everyone wants to join: the exclusive "scratch" club that so few golfers can join. I finally shaved off those last few strokes once I began to understand what caused my inconsistency and could determine drills or lessons to fix them.

Now that I got my sob story out of the way, let's get down to business and get you winning golf matches—whether you want to get even with your buddies who've been beating up on you for years, maybe make it a step further in your club championship this year, or just try to get your handicap down to a respectable number. Whatever your golf goal is, as long as you are patient and truly implement these changes in your golf game, you will no doubt be playing better f*cking golf.

Chapter 3: Your Aim and Alignment Are Off—Way F*cking Off

In this lesson, we will focus on reducing the variable of incorrect aim and alignment. You can make the best swing in the world, but if you're aiming at the pond, guess where it's going? You could also be aligned perfectly to the target, but if your spatial awareness is off and you think the target is 60 yards to the left of where it actually is, hello Slice City.

Think about this for a second: In just about any competitive sport or athletic action, you perform the movement or action with direct visualization of the intended target. It's crazy to think that golf is one of the only—if not *the* only—sport where you aren't looking at your target during the action. Could you imagine if basketball players had to shoot the ball while looking at the floor? Or what if major league pitchers had to close their eyes before they started their windup? Crazy to think about it in that perspective, right? But when we hear about the golf swing, nobody really talks about this aspect.

I say it a lot, and I honestly don't know if there is any science to it, but in my mind, a majority of bad shots are due to bad alignment and swinging to a false target. Well, at least shots that get airborne, anyways. For clarification, what I mean when I say "false target" is that when you are looking at the ball during your swing, you think you know where that target is, right? But if you have never done the drill I will be describing shortly, it's likely that the location you *think* the target is to where it actually is are extremely far from each other. Therefore, you are actually directing your swing to a spot on the course far away from your intended target. It's ok if you're still a little confused at this point (my shitty writing is really starting to shine), you will understand more clearly as I explain the drill in better detail. This problem is so common and goes uncorrected so often, that most golfers just chalk it up to being "part of the game".

This drill alone will probably be a game-changer for quite a few people. It's also why I am talking about it first. I help a lot of fellow golfers with this drill when they "just can't figure out what's going on"—ever think or say that on the golf course before? I can see it now: you make what feels like a great swing, yet the ball does not even come close to your target. You're dumbfounded, and probably throw out a "how in the f*ck did that just happen?" Just know that this is extremely common, and I still struggle with this when I forget to properly line up my shot when I approach the ball.

It may be that one day you're slicing everything, and the next you're hooking everything. Or, the biggest insult to injury, you're playing for your patented slice and you hit the "dreaded straight ball" right in the f*cking trees. I can tell you with confidence – and I can almost guarantee that no golf instructor will - this drill will take care of the "I can't figure it outs." Now, it may not turn you into a better golfer overnight, but once you have this issue figured out, when you hit bad shots—and trust me, you still will—you will at least understand why. Just having the ability to understand *why* will improve your game. Then you can attribute the bad result to a bad swing or some other mechanical issue.

* * *

Here's the f*cking target awareness and alignment drill: Go to bettergolfnow.com and go to **better f*cking**

golf drills to see the video and pictures of this drill. First, pick out a target on the driving range such as a flag, a pole, or something concrete in the ground at about 150-200 yards away. If the target is too close, you won't get legitimate feedback from this drill. Approach the ball like you normally would hit a shot on the course. Take your stance and do everything you normally would before you start your backswing. Now, instead of starting your backswing, righties—take your left hand off the club, and lefties—take your right hand off the club. While keeping your head down and looking at the ball **(don't look up, that's the most important part of this drill!)**, use your pointer finger and extend your arm and point to where you think the target is. Once you feel like you have the target locked in, keeping your arm and finger steady. Take a peek where you are pointing. My guess is you will be shocked at how f*cking far off you are. The first time I did this drill, I was dumbfounded. I've seen people pointing from 60-100 yards left or right of their target, including myself. If you think about this concept, it makes sense why there are times you make a great swing, and the result is not even close to what you're expecting, right?

The tendency for most right-handed golfers is to be aligned right of the target. Meaning, your left shoulder and left hip (opposite for lefties) are pointed to the right of the target. Then when they look down at the ball before they start their swing, they believe the target is even further left than it actually is. This is a recipe for a boomerang slice like you've never seen before and is why most amateurs slice the ball. Like I mentioned before, this was my patented shot before I figured this shit out. I couldn't hit a driver when there were trees down the left side, it was seriously that bad.

Now, there is a second part to this drill that's just as important, and it can be done one of two ways. I recommend trying the first version initially and once you get the hang of it, utilize the second version of this drill. Before you step away from the ball, take the club you were using and place it on the ground with the shaft up against your toes. Once the shaft is on the ground, stand 3-4 feet behind where you were standing and draw an imaginary parallel line where your ball is, with the club laying on the ground. This will show you where your body was aimed when you hit the shot. Once you see the combination of your body not being properly aligned to the target, along with swinging to a false target, you can quickly make sense of the problem. If you slice or hook the ball, you'll be able to see why that's happening very easily. Go to bettergolfnow.com to see a video and pictures of this drill.

Now I will describe the second version of this drill. Once you have done this drill a few times, you can grab a second club and place it down on the ground exactly where your feet should be positioned (parallel line from the ball to the target). Now, when you approach the ball and take your stance, this will properly align you to the target. It will ensure you are aimed correctly and will get your eyes and brain used to seeing where a properly aligned target should be in your peripheral. I would encourage doing this drill almost every time you play for at least a month, especially if your first crack at this drill was just as bad as mine. I know Jordan Spieth lays down his alignment sticks during every single range session before a round. So don't feel like you are an incompetent golfer if you need to do this every time you go to the range. A lot of top PGA Tour golfers utilize alignment drills during every practice session. Also, if you live in a cold weather state like I do and you have to re-learn how to f*cking play golf every April, it's probably a good idea to do all of these drills often in the spring. You can even do them out on the course, if you don't slow up the group behind you (don't be that f*cking guy). If you have time to go to the range, always go to the range. Practicing this drill at the range before your round will train your eyes and brain on correct alignment and swinging to your target will help you when you get out on the course. The best part of this change in your game is that it's not a "swing thought". For clarification, a swing thought is something you remind yourself to do right before you start your swing. Shit, I remember early on, my swing thoughts were atrocious. I would walk up to the ball saying things like "swing nice and easy, shift your weight to the front side, don't look like a f*cking idiot," you name it, I probably reminded myself right before I hit the ball.

Review of how this drill will make you play better f*cking golf:

We removed two variables and made them constant. Body squared to target and swinging to the intended target.

1) It gives you a lot more confidence when standing over the ball, which will encourage better swings and better results

2) It's not a "swing thought," and we all know how dangerous those can be, especially when there are too many floating around in your head. Everything is done before you even start your swing and sets you up for success.

Chapter 4: Keep Your Head F*cking Still, and Your Feet Too

The last chapter focused on the biggest pre-swing variable most amateurs have. This chapter will focus on the biggest intra-swing variable: head movement.

Back in my day as a pitcher at an elite level, I had days where I was spot on and could make the ball dance. Other days when I couldn't find the strike zone to save my life. Not until after my career was over, I realized that I had way too much variability in my pitching delivery. The reason why my results from outing to outing were extremely variable now made a ton of sense. It's no coincidence that my golf game was an almost identical type of situation. There were days I couldn't miss a shot, and others I contemplated walking off the course mid-round. Those were the days you would catch me drinking beers at 8 a.m. Trust me when I say, that's not good for anyone.

A consistent golf swing is all about reducing variables. I will say this again and again, and it coincides with every single lesson is this book: REDUCE VARIABLES. The fewer variables in any motion, the higher the probability of consistency, and in golf, that means good shots. Before I get into the drill description, I want to describe why and how this is so important conceptually. If you assess any pro golfer's head throughout their swing, this is one thing all great golfers do, and they do it really f*cking well. If this isn't a good enough indicator of why it's so important, the practical science behind it should be.

Try this at home with someone, and for f*ck's sake, please use a tennis ball or any type of soft ball. We tried this once with a golf ball, and let's just say that person didn't play stellar golf that day. So instead of inserting a liability disclaimer, I'm just asking you to please use some common sense. Have someone stand 10 feet away from you and toss you a ball underhand and catch it like you normally would. I would bet my mortgage that your head stays perfectly still when you do that; it's innate. Now do the same thing, but this time, I want you to move your head back and forth from shoulder to shoulder fairly quickly (like teaching a baby how to say no) while the other person throws you the ball—and I repeat, a tennis ball! Not so easy to catch the ball, right? This is an exaggerated demonstration, but this is essentially what is happening when your head moves within the golf swing.

Head movement does two things that are detrimental to your golf swing. First, it throws your hand-eye coordination way off. When your head is moving, your vision is compromised. In a game so reliant on hand-eye coordination, you can see why it's so important. Second, it creates a lot of extra body movement (adding another variable) and the wrong kind of body movement. When your head moves backwards, your body sways backwards as well which throws you off balance. Instead, the desired action is to keep your balance and rotate or twist around your steady head. Go ahead and try it for yourself, but usually most people can understand clearly why it's so important to keep your head so steady throughout the entire golf swing. You can also go to bettergolfnow.com to see the video of this drill.

Keeping your head still promotes the twisting or winding motion in the golf swing, which also creates the speed in the swing. I see too many golfers on the range trying to pick up power by swaying or just shifting their weight to their back foot, and their hips barely rotate. When you start this drill, you may feel like you can't get your club very high, and it may feel like you're doing a ¾ swing, but trust me that your swing will still be powerful— and very likely more powerful than before. John Rahm is a great example of this; he has one of the most abbreviated or shortened backswings on tour, yet he is one of the longest hitters on tour.

Again, when your head moves backward as you start your swing, your body sways and shifts your whole body backward. Unless you're able to time moving your head back to where it started in perfect harmony with your downswing, you're either going to chunk the shot (if your head doesn't move back in time) or thin the shot (if your head moves back too quickly). Going back to the tennis ball catching drill, you may still get lucky as hell and catch the ball but it's not nearly as often (reduce f*cking variables). Also, your head moving backward and not twisting or "winding up" takes away so much power it's not even funny. By mastering this skill, you will likely pick up measurable distance in your golf game. And for you serious chunkers, no more biffing in front of the cart girl.

To simplify everything said about head movement: It throws your hand-eye coordination and balance way f*cking off.

We haven't touched on the feet yet but keeping the feet still during the backswing (more technically, keeping your heels on the ground) accomplishes the same goal as keeping your head still. It's all about your balance. These two things work together. Think of them as a package deal if you will. A lot of amateur golfers feel the need to lift their front heel off the ground during the swing. This comes from watching golfers in the 70s, most notably Jack Nicklaus. He was the biggest name in golf at the time and lifted his front heel throughout his career. Naturally, this causes amateurs to think heel lifting is the key to a better game. I'm here to tell you to knock it off.

Here is my best crack at drawing a comparison to an amateur golfer trying to replicate this move. Imagine a Thursday night pickup basketball player trying to shoot a Michael Jordan fadeaway...for his f*cking free throws. It's completely unnecessary and adds so much complexity it's not even close to being worth it. It's an advanced move that will add nominal distance with the high likelihood of much greater inconsistency. What's the benefit of hitting it further if you're not hitting it straight? Aside from the mid-round search parties in the woods, not a damn thing.

Most amateurs feel that lifting the front heel during the backswing will increase power and length in their swing. This is true, but the ability to get that foot back down in time and not throw your balance off all at the same time, is really hard to do. This makes it counterproductive in every aspect. Most importantly, it encourages your head to move backward and puts your body in a compromised position from where you started. There are still some tour pros who utilize this move, but they are definitely an exception to the rule. It's also somewhat unlikely that you'll see them making a run at the title on Sunday afternoons.

You also have golfers that lift their back heel before contact is made. Justin Thomas is the most notable pro who does this well, but again, he is the exception to the rule. Most guys on tour leave their back heel down until after contact is made. The main reason I don't recommend this is that it again adds complexity to the swing and another variable. As amateur golfers, we are all just trying to hit the ball straight. Sure, we want to hit it farther, but I think we could all agree that fairways and greens are much more fun no matter what clubs you hit to accomplish that.

Simply put, keeping both heels planted through impact is your best bet at increased consistency. After impact, your body will be moving so fast and uncoiling (assuming you kept your f*cking head still) that your back heel will have no choice but to lift off the ground. *After* the ball is hit lifting the back heel is fine and is obviously a signature pose for all golfers. The issue lies when the foot is lifted as a tool for hitting the ball further, rather than as a result of momentum after the ball is hit. If you can try to keep that heel planted as close to impact as possible, you will greatly benefit from reducing another major variable: shitty balance.

If you lift the front heel, you need to get that heel planted again before you make impact. This is no doubt a variable, and a major one at that. If that heel doesn't hit the ground at the perfect time, it's highly unlikely you're going to hit a good shot. Why? Try hitting balls on the range with your front heel off the ground the entire time. Actually, please don't try that. You'll probably end up missing every ball you swing at and that is just embarrassing. The reality is that the heel lift encourages and produces so many more negatives than any positives it could produce. If you have countless hours to practice like many tour pros, yeah, the heel lift might help you get a better turn and maybe a few more yards. In the sense of an amateur golf game, most of us are just trying to hit more than two f*cking fairways a round, so take my word on this one. More distance with more variability, is just having to look further into the woods for your ball.

* * *

Here's the f*cking head still and feet still drill:

There are three ways to practice this drill. All have their advantages.

Go to <u>bettergolfnow.com</u> and go to **better f*cking golf drills** to see the video and pictures of this drill.

1) The first way is to utilize a product I made from necessity to practice this drill by myself on the range. The product is currently in the working prototype phase and I am currently having it tested around the country. It's called the **Tour Balance™**

Golf Swing Aid available for purchase on Amazon and on bettergolfnow.com very soon. It's very inexpensive, lightweight and the best part is you can leave it in your golf bag during a round (shameless plug). If you're listening to this book and can't see the pictures on the website, I will do my best to describe what the device looks like.

The device sticks into the ground, and you adjust the telescopic pole to your correct height. It comes with an alignment stick along with a foam stick. The telescopic pole has an adapter that can rotate and lock at any angle from 180-degrees to 90-degrees. You want the tip of the foam or alignment stick right next to your ear/head (for right-handers, you hold it next to your right ear, and left-handers, hold it next to your left ear) Now, just perform a golf swing without moving your head. You'll know immediately if your head moves, as you will feel your head/ear touch the foam or stick. The immediate feedback here is great, it allows you to perform the swing without consciously thinking about moving your head. Although, if this is a serious problem you have with your swing, it may take some conscious effort initially before it becomes natural. You may even notice that you have no problem keeping your head still during the back swing. But when you start the downswing, your head is moving backwards. This is something that can very easily go unnoticed and without this device, it will go uncorrected. This again just takes time and practice to correct before it becomes something you can perform without even thinking about it. If you are interested in getting your hands on this product before it is commercially available, email me at info@bettergolfnow.com.

2) The second way is simple and won't cost a dime, but you will need someone with you while you practice (which, as we know, is not ideal or feasible most of the time). Simply take your golf stance and have someone stand on the opposite side of the ball from you (you are essentially facing each other if you were both standing). The person picks the longest club in your bag and holds the grip right next to your ear (for right-handers, they're holding it next to your right ear and left-handers holding it

next to your left ear). Now, just perform a golf swing without moving your head. This provides the exact same feedback as the **Tour Balance™ Golf Swing Aid** (second shameless plug) but requires someone with you who is dedicated to helping you through multiple swings and has a steady arm.

3) The third way is to simply focus on your head movement while you practice. I only recommend this if the other two options are not available, as this creates a swing thought and takes the focus off everything else you are trying to do in your swing. Also, there are a lot of times your head can move, and you do not even realize it. This is good for practice swings within a round or a quick warmup session on the range before a round. But ideally, you want to not have to think about anything while you swing and only receive feedback if something is off.

Here's the f*cking feet still drill:

Take two household sponges. It doesn't matter the size of the sponge. Get them nice and wet and strain them out a few times until they make noise when compressed. Put them under your heels. If you lift either heel throughout the swing, you'll hear a squish. It's that easy. You should never hear a sound from the front heel throughout the entire swing, and from the back heel, you will hear a sound right before impact or right at impact if you are doing it correctly.

Review of how this drill will make you play better f*cking golf:

We again removed two variables and made them constant. Head movement and feet/heel movement.

1) Keeping your head still will be the biggest game changer you can make in your golf swing. Hands down, in any hand-eye coordination sport or activity, if your head is moving, it's a hell of a lot harder to do it. Simple as that. If you still don't understand the importance of keeping your head still, send me an email at **ihatehittingfairwaysandgreens@stopreadingthisbookno w.com**.

2) Keeping your heels on the ground throughout the swing will again create more consistency and better balance. It will also promote and ensure (when coupled

with no head movement) a winding and un-winding movement which will create power and speed.

Chapter 5: Keep Your Head (and Eyes) Down after Impact . . . Like, Way After Impact . . . Even F*cking Longer

As the old saying goes, if I had a dollar for every f*cking time people look at me after duffing a shot, looking dumbfounded about what the hell just happened—well, I wouldn't be trying to sell books that's for damn sure. I've seen people pull their heads up almost simultaneously with their downswing. When I tell them that, they look at me like I'm crazy. I often get something like, "there is no way that's what just happened," or "I swear my head was down that time,". Listen Karen, you were looking at the f*cking moon when the club contacted the ball. Even good golfers I play with still struggle with this and may not even realize it's the issue (including myself, being one of those golfers every f*cking April when I re-learn how to play golf in the damn snow).

I've thought about this problem in amateur golfers a lot. I have been trying to figure out why it's so hard for most people to accomplish this. It's one of those things in golf that no one really understands, so no one really talks about it. It's kind of like checking the fridge, seeing there's no food, and then checking it again five minutes later. We've all done it, but literally have no f*cking idea why. This is one part of the golf swing I've had to dig deep to find answers. After some serious digging, I believe the answer comes from two concepts. First, and what we will focus the majority of the time on, our brain function and Acute Stress Response (ASR). This is more commonly known as "fight or flight" response. Second, understanding how the club shaft flexes during the swing and where your club head is in relation to your hands when you contact the ball. All right so here is your warning: please bear with me, it's impossible to explain ASR without getting a little nerdy.

Simply speaking, if we can comprehend how our brains work and why they work the way that they do, it will be easier to correct a behavior or habit. As humans in today's world, our ASR is so underutilized that our brains find ways to make use of it in order to keep it finely tuned for real emergencies. We aren't getting chased down by tigers just outside our caves anymore, and we sure as hell aren't worried about sneaking up on a big ass buffalo for our next meal. I think we can all agree that for most of us, our once daily need for our ASR is no longer. Because of this it takes something as simple as a meeting with your boss, a presentation you have to give to a small group, or in this case, the fear of hitting a bad shot to be triggered. Consider your ASR as the mall security guard that takes their job way too seriously, and when they see a kid with a water gun, they walkie-talkie their partner in for backup. Simply speaking, our lives are not that difficult anymore, but our brains aren't ready to adapt to the laziness. Probably soon though at this rate.

ASR is essentially a stress signal in your brain when you perceive or recognize danger, threat, crisis, or emergency. When our brains are in "fight-or-flight mode," we can subconsciously predict things that are about to happen to give us time to react. **This is the first major aspect to this concept**. In the world of golf, this will help you understand why it's so hard to keep your head down during the swing (obviously the most important thing to understand in life). The brain's ability to predict *what's about to happen* is why it's so easy to lift your head before you've contacted the ball. Your brain is telling you the contact has already been made, even though it hasn't yet. So, if you're ever stepping into a shot that puts you out of your comfort zone and the consequences of a bad shot are high ($200 bet on the line anyone?) here comes Paul Blart the Mall Cop, ready to f*ck your shit up. At this point, your hypothalamus (the brain's crisis center) is turned on. It's also important to note that, as changes in the body begin to happen, they happen so quickly that most people are unaware they are even happening. Your blood pressure goes up, adrenaline enters your bloodstream, your pupils dilate, and your senses become heightened and narrowly focused. It has been shown in studies that this process and our brains are so efficient, these things happen before our visual centers have time to process what is happening. Cue getting to the f*cking point of why this mumbo-jumbo is important for your golf game.

In golf, what are possible fears we may encounter? Hitting a bad shot that ruins your round, right? Maybe being embarrassed in front of your playing partners on the first tee box or maybe a fear of bystanders watching as you swing on the range or on the course. I can't even tell you how many bad golf swings I've seen in front of the cart girl. Just relax dude. If you give her a good tip and don't ask her what she's doing later, she doesn't give a shit how you hit. No matter what shot makes you uncomfortable, the higher the stakes for a bad shot, the higher likelihood your brain will go into fight-or-flight mode without you even realizing it. You might be thinking, "OK cool. Now how do I stop it from f*cking happening?". It's as simple as exaggerating and practicing an action to make it an automated response in a time of stress. Similar to why people take self-defense classes or practice emergency action plans. The more you practice something, the less likely it is you will have to think about it when your brain locks into ASR mode.

The golf swing takes just over one second from start to finish. This drill I'm about to describe is an exaggeration of maybe a tenth of a second, but once you practice it, it will feel like an eternity. Just try to remember that your brain will be in a much more heightened state on the par-3 17th at TPC Sawgrass (for those of you living under a rock, that's the iconic island green surrounded by water) than it will be for a layup shot on a par-5 with a pitching wedge in your hand. Even less still when hitting your 10th straight-eight iron on the range with a cigar in your mouth. In short, the exaggeration will feel much more or less extreme based on which type of shot you're hitting.

Okay, so let's assume you've bought into this concept now, but the next question lingering in your mind is, "Wait, what if by the time I look up I don't know where my ball is, I can't track its flight, and I just lost a ball for no reason?" Well, first off, when is the last time you ever played alone and nobody was watching your ball with you? The next question naturally is, "What if the other people in my group are talking and not paying attention to my shot?" Fair point. Going back to the original idea of this concept, the exaggeration only lasts a tenth of a second or likely even less. The average hang time for most shots is about 6 seconds (give or take). It is highly likely (unless you REALLY exaggerate staring at the ground) you will look up in plenty of time to see where your shot ends up. Once you practice this on the range, you'll figure out quickly that leaving your eyes and head down even after the ball is gone doesn't affect your ability to follow your shot in the air. It's one of those things that you have to experience for yourself to fully understand and trust the method. Furthermore, it's a hell of a lot easier to find a ball that is in the fairway because you kept your f*cking head still than it is a shank into the fescue because you tried to see it before you hit it, am I right?

Ok shit, that was a lot on brain function. In order to understand why keeping your head down is important, you have to first understand how the club shaft flexes during the swing. If you're an experienced golfer, it's likely you have a clear understanding that there is a flex built into each golf club. But even for experienced golfers, this is a good reminder. For anyone reading this that's a novice golfer, take a club out of your bag and wiggle it quickly back and forth. You will see how the shaft flexes. Try it out with a pitching wedge, a 7-iron, a 4-iron and then your driver. You will see that each club has a different type of flex mostly attributed to the length of the club. Magnify the flex you see when you do this by two to three times and you will have a good idea of what it looks like when you take a full swing. So, what the f*ck does this have to do with keeping my head down you ask? When the club face hits the ball during the swing, your hands are actually in front of the ball when you make contact (if you effectively use the 50% rule which we will dive into next chapter). So, if you are looking up when you *think* you have hit the ball, you may actually be looking up way too f*cking early.

The longer the club the more your club shaft flexes during the swing. That means your hands will be that much further in front of the ball when contact is made. Your brain's ASR is going nuts and you are anticipating the club making contact with the ball. Because of this heightened state of awareness, your senses will be slightly ahead of what is actually happening. It now makes a lot of sense why it's so easy to be looking at the f*cking clouds when the club hits the ball, right? The ASR likely accounts for a tenth of a second and the club shaft flex accounts for another tenth of a second. When you combine these two with the average swing taking one second, you're probably lifting your head when you've only finished 80% of your swing. It also should leave you with a better understanding of why when you start to practice this drill, it feels like you're keeping your eyes and head down for a f*cking eternity.

Here's the f*cking head and eyes down drill:

There are a lot of ways to practice this, but these are the two best ways that I've found that don't distract you from your swing and ultimately create other bad habits. With both drills, I want you to tell yourself to keep swinging the club to the target well after the ball is gone. **Just remember, it may feel like the ball is gone and you made contact forever ago, but that is your ASR predicting and anticipating that makes it feel that way.**

1) The best drill is simply to leave your head and eyes down and staring at the ball (or, where the ball was) until the motion of your body and your right shoulder (left shoulder if you're a lefty) hits your chin and forces your head up. This is an easy way to keep your head down and avoid having to guess or manipulate when it's time to pick your head up and look at your ball in flight. Another way to think of this is, when you feel the club head and both arms fully extended to the target, then it's time to look up.

2) Another way to practice this drill is to continue to keep your eyes down until you can see a full divot, or the ball has disappeared. This one is good if you're more of a "visual" learner versus a "feel" learner. This allows you to take a visual cue on when it's time to look up vs. a feeling of your right shoulder pushing your chin up or your arms fully extended to the target.

Try both and see what works best for you. Also keep in mind, this is both important and effective for every single club in your bag, especially your putter! But I can guarantee that if you understand the science behind this concept and implement the drill (even if it feels like an extreme exaggeration), your ball striking and putting ability will increase tenfold.

Review of how this drill will make you play better f*cking golf:

We removed a single variable here, but another big one: keeping your head down after impact. Even for good golfers, this is still a critical drill to work on for better ball striking.

1) Understanding how your brain works when you face an important shot allows you to realize that what feels like an exaggeration of keeping your head down *well after impact* is actually keeping your head down likely *right until impact.*

2) If you're not looking at the ball at impact, it's a hell of a lot harder to make good contact. I will repeat, keep your head down after impact, then even f*cking longer.

Chapter 6: 50% Rule—Stop Trying to F*cking Kill It, It's Counterproductive

Tell me if you've heard something along these lines before: "I was hitting so well on the range, and then I got out on the course and couldn't f*cking figure it out." Or maybe something like, "I'm coming up short on everything today; I just don't get it." My favorite is, "Did that really go over the green? I barely swung at it."

Sorry dude, just because you hit an eight-iron 180 yards one time on a downhill par-3 with the wind at your back does not officially make your 8-iron your 180-yard club. This is an exaggeration, but most amateur golfers definitely overestimate how far they can hit their clubs. They don't consider the wind, elevation, and temperature when accessing the results of the shot. Also, swinging harder does not mean the ball will go further. I repeat, *harder does not mean further.* Imagine me at the top of the Swiss Alps with a massive alphorn and instead of shouting "Ricola" I'm yelling "slow the f*ck down".

I bet you can think about someone you play with, and it's the same person with the most beautiful and tempo-rich practice swings, but then when they step up to the ball, it's like someone injected them with a deadly combination of caffeine and steroids. I get it, though—when the guys on TV like Jason Day, Justin Thomas, Rory McIlroy, and Tiger all seem like they're swinging with all of their might, well, they are. You also must remember they're not only professionals but also the best in the game. They practice for hundreds of hours a month, and the variables in their swing are almost nonexistent. For them, increased speed does not create increased variability. For the other 99.9% of golfers in the world, **increased speed IS increased variability and therefore, adds massive amounts of inconsistency**.

As you could imagine, it gets worse the higher your handicap is. So, the biggest question I want you to ask yourself is, what do you consider to be a successful round of golf? Is it when you hit your driver the furthest in your group (so what if it had a 60-yard slice and ended up in someone's backyard)? Or is it when you posted a low score, or even the lowest ever? I really hope you f*cking answered the latter. So, why do most of us get so caught up in the distance? I don't know about you guys, but when I stick a 150-yard approach shot tight, I'm damn happy. Does it really matter if it was a 9-iron or a 6-iron?

If I told you that the same reason you're picking your head up too early is the same reason you're swinging too hard, would you be surprised? It's the same part of your brain being tapped into without you even knowing it. It can come from a fear of choosing the wrong club and not having the distance to get it there. Maybe you felt the wind pick up just as you pulled the club away or you have second thoughts on the club choice. The most annoying one for me is if something distracts me during my swing (a bug flying around my ball, my shadow, some idiot un-velcroed their glove). No matter what the reason is, harder does not mean further. Again, our fight-or-flight response (that mall cop ready to chase down someone who parked illegally in the parking lot) is so underutilized these days it kicks in for the slightest sense of urgency or fear and almost always before you even have time to realize it's happening.

The biggest issue at hand here is that "harder" for most amateurs means more arms, more hands, and more upper body. All this does is slows the club down and causes major variability in the swing, which by now I hope you understand is not a f*cking good thing. By overutilizing your arms and hands, you take away the ability for the club shaft to flex and snap through the ball, which is where the real power comes from. This is how older guys on the senior tour are still able to hit the ball 300 yards. They rotate their bodies around their perfectly still head and let their lower body take the bulk of the swing. This allows the club to bend or flex the maximum amount for distance. So, what's the solution? The 50% rule.

The 50% rule is something that I've experimented with multiple playing partners over the years. It's as simple as it sounds: just take a 50% swing at the ball and hit the club longer than you normally would. When you're on the course, if the stakes are high with a big Nassau, or maybe you're playing decent today and you're going for a personal record. The ASR part of your brain kicks in and adrenaline levels become high. However, with an understanding that speed creates variability and ultimately inaccuracy, what do you think will create a better shot? A one hundred fifty percent 8-iron that's hit off-center of the clubface, or a fifty percent 7-iron hit right in the middle of the clubface? The reality of the 50% rule is that you're not actually swinging at 50%, you're probably at 100% swing speed rather than the 250% you were at previously. The idea is to tell yourself you're only swinging 50% to allow you to slow down and let the club naturally flex through the hitting zone. Rather than forcing the club through the hitting zone with your arms, the lower body takes over and the club flexes like it's supposed to, allowing for much better contact. It also creates more calmness and confidence that you'll hit a better shot. From what I've seen in my friendly experiments over the years, what usually happens is that within the first few times they try it, it works well. They will see the improvement immediately, which is ultimately the instant reward the brain needs to continue to do anything.

I will warn you that there is a fine line here. The 50% rule gets easily mistaken with the "lazy swing" rule, and that's where things go awry. Fifty percent effort turns into 50% body control, 50% balance, 50% follow-through and honestly, 50% shits-given for the shot in general. This lesson or skill is simply designed to allow you to see that consistency comes from better contact. Better contact comes from having more control of your club. More control of your club comes from not over-swinging with your upper body and arms. So, even though this lesson is the easiest to comprehend and likely the easiest to implement into your game, it still requires practice and patience.

* * *

Here's the f*cking 50% rule drill: Once you're nice and warmed up (seriously, don't hurt yourself), grab a long iron or a driver. It's sometimes easy to get away with over-swinging the shorter irons, and you get much better feedback from the longer clubs with this drill. Your first few swings will be your normal speed swing. Get a good gauge on where the ball lands and ultimately comes to rest in terms of distance and accuracy. The next 3 swings will be long drive champion swings. I mean, I want you to give this thing a f*cking whack. Assess the shot and take note of the distance and accuracy compared to your normal swing. If it so happens, they're further and more accurate, just remember you're on the range hot shot and not on the course with a big bet on the line and trees lining the fairway. Your next 3 swings will be your 20% swing speed. I want you to think like you broke every club in your bag except you driver and your putter, and you must hit a layup shot on a par 5. Make sure you're still completing a full downswing, just at 20% speed. Really try to concentrate on feeling and controlling the clubface. Your last 3 swings will be your 50% swing. You should have a noticeably clear picture in your mind what it feels like to swing like a long drive champion along with swinging with little effort. This is where you find that perfect balance and find your true tempo. I encourage you to eventually do this with every club in your bag, even your putter. Once you have a feel of both extremes, you're capable of finding your balanced swing. The basic concept of not too hot, not too cold, just right. Good work Goldilocks.

Review of how this drill will make you play better f*cking golf:

We removed a single variable here, but another big one: inconsistency caused by swinging too hard.

1) Understanding how real swing speed is created (club flexing or snapping through the ball and not Hulk Hogan arms) will allow you to be able to embrace the 50% rule as your go-to swing.

2) The 50% rule does not mean you're swinging at 50% speed. The rule allows you to take the effort out of your arms and hands and let the power come from the shaft flexing and snapping through the ball.

Chapter 7: Change What Part of the Ball You Look At—You'll Be Amazed at the F*cking Results

I would say my favorite question I get on the course is usually right after I hit a greenside pitch from a tight fairway lie that checks once and comes to a dead stop: "How in the hell do you hit that shot?" I usually follow up with, "When you look at the ball, what part of the ball do you look at?" The most common response is, "I don't even know, I just look at the ball." The close seconds are "the back of the ball" or "the center of the ball." When I tell them that I look at the front of the ball, they usually give me a look that says, "The f*ck?"

The answer is much more simplistic than most would think (assuming you have a wedge with clean grooves, and you are playing a tour style golf ball). I focus my eyes at the front of the golf ball and just swing smooth. DISCLAIMER: If you focus your eyes on the back of the ball, try baby steps with this technique, as going from the back to the front will likely feel too extreme. Maybe start at focusing on the center of the ball, and eventually move to the front. Now, I'm not going to lie, I am oversimplifying this just a tad. It still takes more practice before you can pull this shot off on the course, but just shifting your focus to the part of the golf ball closest to the target makes a world of difference, and this is not for just short game shots but across your entire bag. So why the f*ck does where I look at the ball change my shot? Once again, it all about tricking your brain.

If we look back at the lessons we have learned so far, aside from Chapter 4—**Keep your Head F*cking Still, and Your Feet Too**—all the lessons are essentially ways to "trick" your brain or re-train your brain to get a desired result. This is no different. This is one lesson I learned from trial and error, and although I never watched or heard a professional talk about this, I would assume some or most good golfers do the same.

There are three contacts that you can make. In a simplified manner, you can make proper contact, you can hit it thin (a low line-drive that barely gets off the ground), or you can hit it fat (where you hit so much turf before the ball that the ball hardly goes anywhere). Also, for all of you who like to drink *a lot* on the golf course, take me down to the Chunky City, where the divots are thick, and the girls think you're shitty. Yeah, that was a bad joke, but I can't get that song out of my head when I see a massive divot flying further than the ball; it just seems too perfect.

Let's start off by answering this question: why do thin shots happen? I could give you the scientific golf magazine answer, but it would leave you frustrated and no better off than before you read the article. I could go on and on about golf articles and their over-descriptive rationale for the golf swing. They just confuse everyone to the point where they have no choice but to keep on watching or buy another magazine, right? Guilty as charged. But we all know the real reason: it's the fear of chunking it, probably the most embarrassing and irritating thing you can do on the golf course. So, we overcompensate and try to "pick it clean", "lift the ball" and swing up at it rather than down through the ball. But when we look at it mechanically, it is usually caused by the head movement towards the sky on your downswing. This causes your arms and body to lift, which doesn't allow the club to return to where it started at your set up. So, no, Acme Golf Magazine, it's not because you over-pronated your pinky finger two degrees before contact that caused the thin shot. It's definitely not because your swing plane was compromised due to the lack of centrifugal force when your hips over-rotated. You hit it thin cause you didn't want to chunk it, it's that f*cking simple.

Okay, so we figured out why thin shots happen; but how and why do fat/chunked shots happen? These are usually caused by someone who moves their head backward during the backswing. They cannot get their head back to where it was at setup before the club reaches the ball. If your head doesn't get back in time, the point at which your club shallows out will be that much further behind the ball. When you couple this with someone who focuses their eyes on the backside of the ball, it's a recipe for a lot of chunked shots throughout the day. In contrast to thinned shots, it can also be cause by someone who is moving their head closer to the ground in their swing, causing their club to hit the ground well behind the ball from their setup.

Okay, so I'm about to talk about the swing arc for a bit. I know, I know, I said I wouldn't go there. It's not my

MO to talk about swing mechanics, nor is it my goal to change them. However, I do think having a basic understanding of what is happening in your swing helps make sense of why you want to focus your eyes on the front of the ball. I'm sure most of you have heard this before, but any good golfer contacts the ball first and the ground second. When I say this to most amateur golfers, they still do not trust and/or understand this concept. They feel that in order to hit the ball first, they must "pick it clean" while contacting the ball as the club is on the upward trajectory of its arc.

Go to bettergolfnow.com, and under the images tab (and if you're listening, I'll try my best to explain). You can see a divot made after a par-3 shot where the ball was on a tee. There is about ½" to 1" of un-touched turf in front of the tee and then the start of a normal looking divot. How is this possible? The only way this can happen is if the clubhead is still traveling at a downward angle after contact is made. Where a lot of amateurs get caught up, is they're trying to "smack" or "slap" the ball with their club, as opposed to the desired "crunch" or "squish" of the ball. A golf ball is 1.5" from front to back. Assuming you have the ball in the center of your stance with a mid-iron or short-iron, by shifting your eyes to the front of the ball, you're tricking your brain into bottoming out your swing at the front of the ball.

When looking at the front of the ball, even if your contact is not perfect, it will be near impossible to hit a chunk or fat shot. That 1 1/2" is a big distance in the grand scheme of things, especially considering someone who is currently trying to pick the ball clean off the fairway. Everyone likes to say it's a game of inches. The reality is it's a game of millimeters, and by focusing your eyes and brain 38mm in front of where you have been looking, you will instantly change your ball contact from an ascending blow to a descending blow. This creates more backspin on your ball, so it doesn't hit the green and run for days. The added backspin also produces much higher trajectories and distance so that you're hitting shorter clubs on your approach shots.

* * *

Here's the f*cking look at the front of the ball drill:

Go to the short game area or the practice green (if your golf club allows chipping on the practice green). I would start in the normal rough and eventually work up to a tight lie off the first cut/fairway. Once you develop a feel for this technique and build up some confidence, you can start to use it for every club in your bag. Now, take the most lofted club you have in your bag and practice hitting 15-20-yard chip shots. Keep your focus on the front of the ball and ensure you are contacting the ball as the club is descending, rather than ascending. It's important to not force the club into the ball or "chop" at the ball when you are doing this. This is an action amateurs' use to help prevent chunking the shot. When you focus on the front of the ball, you no longer need to worry about that. Just take a nice smooth (think 50% rule) swing at it, but with a downward trajectory at the front of the ball and watch for yourself. It may take some time before you start seeing it come off the club consistently, so have some f*cking patience here. But the goal is get used to this with the short shots and then start practicing it with your 9-iron and eventually move up to your driver. I put this drill/lesson last for a reason, as it's likely the toughest to implement but will ultimately give you the best results overall in the sense of consistent ball striking.

Review of how this drill will make you play better f*cking golf:

Another variable we are trying to eliminate here is inconsistent contact due to where your eyes are focused on the ball.

1) Looking at the front of the ball trains your brain to see the front of the ball as the bottom of your swing arc, as opposed to the back of your ball.

2) By focusing on the front of the ball and making it the bottom of your swing path, it will create a greater sense of confidence that you won't hit a fat shot and will allow you to confidently hit down through the golf ball and "trap" it so you properly utilize the grooves on the club to create backspin, higher trajectory shots, and increased distance.

Chapter 8: Stop F*cking Keeping Score . . . Well, Not Literally

All right, before you throw this book in the pond on 18, just give me a chance on this one and you might actually be surprised. I can probably guess what most of you are thinking: "F*ck this guy and the golf cart he rode in on." So, full disclosure, this lesson and the mental approach to golf deserves its own book. Sports phycologists have built careers on the mental aspects of the game. But I also believe in the *KISS* or *keep-it-simple-stupid* attitude, essentially the overall approach of the lessons in this book. So, keeping this topic to a single chapter might be what's best for some of you. If you're into taking a deep dive on learning the best mental approach to the game, I recommend reading *The Unstoppable Golfer* by Bob Rotella. Bob is a genius when it comes to the mental approach to the game, and I listen to this book at least twice a year. It really helps me keep my mental approach strong. Which, as we know, is about 85% of the f*cking game.

Let me throw a few scenarios at you. Do you ever step up to the tee and say something like, "Okay, all I have to do is make a (insert any comfortable or usual type of score) here and I win this bet, match or tournament"? Or how about when somewhere in the middle of one of your best rounds ever you have a major blowup hole (or two) that royally f*cks your entire round. Last, have you ever started a round with two or three awful holes, and then somehow had a stretch of holes well above your skill level? I can almost guarantee we have all had these scenarios happen on the course, and if you're an avid golfer, they happen all too often.

I'll throw one more scenario at you that will really beat this dead horse. Have you ever been in a "do-or-die" type situation with maybe a friendly bet on the line and you must make a near-impossible score on the next hole to win or tie? Maybe it's a birdie on a hole you've never birdied before, or maybe it's par on the toughest hole on the course. When you're put in these situations, isn't it interesting that you always seem to at least have a chance at the score you're going for? No matter how out of reach, and if you fall short, it's dramatically "just short" or "so close"? After the hole, you get the old, "But hey, that's still a great score on this hole" comment from a playing partner. Cue the "hey thanks, f*ck you" half smile and nod.

This lesson is just another way of tricking our brains into getting the desired result we are looking for. If this were a kumbaya inspirational type book I would quote Norman Vincent Peale right here: "Shoot for the moon. Even if you miss, you'll land among the stars." Since I'm not your mommy, I personally prefer "fake it 'till you make it". Either way, this is a quick and dirty breakdown of the mental aspects of the game and another lesson to take out on the course.

The lessons I talk about in this book, with lots of practice and patience, will help your consistency and improve your game. Now, if you're a 15+ handicap and you go out there and say, "I'm going to shoot a 72 today," there is no doubt you're setting yourself up for failure. First off, I don't mind stretch goals, but keep it f*cking real bro. Secondly, you have now engrained a final score into your head, and you've created a situation where you are hyper-focused on the "final score" mentality. If you are the type of person that will not quit until you get there, maybe that's the right strategy for you. Hey, if you fall short, you may fall short with still your best round ever. But for the average golfer it's best to just say f*ck it for now since you will likely just get more pissed with every stroke above your goal.

Being within your comfort zone in terms of your golf score is the ultimate goal. By definition, a comfort zone is a place or situation where one feels safe or at ease and without stress. For me, my comfort zone is two under to three over. For a ten handicapper, it might be a six over to twelve over. No matter what your handicap or skill level is, we all have a score in mind that when we leave the course, we don't want to chuck our clubs out the f*cking window on the drive home. The concept of the comfort zone is not amazingly profound, but attempting to trick your brain into thinking you don't have one is hard as shit. This is golf in a damn nutshell. For anyone who is on pace to shatter their scoring record, there's no chance in hell you are at ease and without stress. Nor is anyone whose round so far is in the toilet they start taking tequila shots by themselves at 8 am. So how do you trick your brain into believing you are in your comfort zone when you actually f*cking aren't?

Imagine this: you have the front nine of your life, and you think "Wow, if I can replicate that or even just have a mediocre back nine, I will post a personal best." We all know how that story ends. A hosel rocket appears out of nowhere, some asshat yells to his buddy on the next hole in your backswing, or you snap hook a ball OB when you've been hitting a fade/slice all day. This is unproven, but it's been said that cart girls have a sixth sense for blowup holes and manage to find you when you're at your low point.

One of two things can happen here. A. You continue on your path of destruction and your stress level goes through the roof. Or B. You stop giving a f*ck because you figure you can't be saved. You give in to the booze and declare yourself the worst golfer in the entire f*cking world. You stop trying to win. Unlike other more aggressive contact sports, stop trying so damn hard is exactly the advice you need at this point. Just like blindly swinging to the target is unique to golf, so is this. Disclaimer: please don't do less in most other sports when you feel stressed or start to lose. It won't work and you might ultimately end up injured.

"Do less- do better" is just another aspect of golf that makes it great. The pressure of performing within your comfort zone is now long gone, and the focus is no longer on the "final score" mentality. It's almost like you go into "driving range mode". See the ball, hit the ball. Zero f*cks given. Which is actually what you should be doing in the first f*cking place (insert 50% rule)! Easier said than done obviously and it's not a place that many can get to even in the pros. But it is exactly where the average Joe Schmo golfer needs to be to find success on the course. Over the years I have come up with a few strategies to try to cope with this ultimate mind f*ck. How do you try to not care when you actually do? For me it started with pitching and translated to golf. Certain times it will be almost impossible, but I think there are some tricks that can help to at least reduce the stress long enough to give you a mental edge on the course. Or at the very least, make the experience more f*cking fun.

Regardless of how the round is going, inevitably your awareness kicks in, and you think about the possibility of what could go wrong on any given shot. Oh, Adam Scott, I hope you're not reading this and painfully reliving the bogeys on 15, 16, 17, and 18 at the British Open to lose by 1 in 2012. I feel your pain man. If only you could've thrown a few back on national television during a major championship. This is one of many examples, we've seen it happen time and time again, and even in other major sports. The "just don't f*ck this up" mentality kicks in. This is like watching a slow-motion train wreck that for some reason, cannot be stopped. The difference is that in other sports, adrenaline and max effort is a good thing. In golf, as we have learned, it's a recipe for f*cking disaster. As with any sport we have been conditioned to focus on the final score or the end result. This is what everyone asks about in the bar after the round. It's what you post in GHIN to determine your handicap, and what golf announcers talk about in broadcasts throughout a tournament. It's nearly impossible to avoid it, but what we can do is at least try to block it out *while* we are playing.

Think about the course you play the most often. I'm sure you know your career-best front nine score and your career-best back nine score, right? Even if you don't know exactly, you have a pretty good idea. If you added up the front and back, I'm willing to bet you're well under your comfort zone. It's also likely that these two personal bests were right before and right after 9-hole scores well above your comfort zone, right? It's harder to remember those 9s, but I would say it's more likely than not. So, what's the takeaway here? You are perfectly capable of putting up a good score, you just have to get out of your own f*cking head about it.

* * *

Here's the stop f*cking keeping score drill: Next time you go out to play, try your best to leave the scorekeeping to someone else in the group. If that's not possible, it's going to take more self-control not to track your score, but it's still doable. After each hole, tally up the scores for the hole and immediately forget them. I know it seems difficult, and it definitely can be if you're playing well, but it's actually easier than you think. The most difficult part is staying committed to it throughout the round. Having the self-control not to look back really quick and add up your scores and figure out where you stand goes against every competitive fiber you have. This will take some time, and honestly, I still struggle with this. With this step, we have removed one scoring goal, probably the most important one, but there is a close second.

The next step removes scoring goals for each hole and looks at each shot as its own task or goal. I want you to look at every shot you have as someone challenging you or (for a degenerate like me) betting you. If you have to, bet $5 with your partner. But what the f*ck Paul, doesn't betting increase your ASR? Not if it's a low risk bet el-cheapo. Shifting your focus to one shot at a time puts your mission only on the shot ahead and nothing else. Focusing on the positive result of each shot takes away the pressure of the overall score. Same goes for a negative outcome. Bad tee shot? No big deal if you are already mentally moved on to the "winning" the next shot. Splitting up the game into shots rather than holes gives you enough of a mental break to calm the f*ck down and reset.

At the risk of sounding cliché, I won't say that positivity is the key to success here. But it kind of f*cking is. For anyone that's stepped up to the ball with a self-talk of "don't hook it into the water on the left" or "stay away from the OB markers on the right," you've now taken a negative approach and target to your swing. Most of us know how that ends up. It's amazing how the ball knows exactly what the f*ck you are thinking.

So, let's walk through your typical par-4 and how it would look with this shot-by-shot mental approach.

- For your tee shot, your mission is to hit the fairway. Only hit a club you know you will hit the fairway with 80%+ certainty. Act as if someone bet you $1,000 you can't hit the fairway. I can almost guarantee you aren't pulling out your driver and saying "f*ck it." This may mean dropping down to iron on a par-4 or par-5, but honestly, what puts you in a better position to make a good score? A driver 250+ in the trees or an iron 180 yards, sitting right in the fairway? So, grab that 4-iron, give it a "watch this," and now you're sitting' pretty in the fairway while you help your playing partners look for their drives in the weeds.

- On your second shot, the challenge or mission is now hitting the green. If the pin is tucked in the corner or back of the green, only go pin hunting if you're 80% positive you can hit the green even if you go right after it. If not, aim for the center of the green and tell your cart partner you'll grab their putter for them as they flip you the bird on their way to their ball in the bunker. This is one of my favorite flexes on the course, by the way. **Better F*cking Subtle Intimidation** should be in bookstores soon. If you're not 80% positive you can hit the green, utilize the 50% rule, and take a nice easy swing with a longer club. In the worst-case scenario, you'll be right around the green and ready to chip in or make an easy par.

- If you don't hit the green, no big deal— but this is a critical point on each hole. I don't care what your handicap is. You could be a 30 handicap for all I care. The only thing you should be telling yourself when you're within 30 yards of the hole is: I'm getting the ball in hole on this next shot.

At this point you're probably thinking "I'm lucky if I make solid contact half the time, how in the hell am I supposed to try to make it in the hole 30 yards out?". There are too many times when a high handicapper approaches a pitch shot and is thinking "Don't chunk this one," or "Don't blade this 30-yards past the green,". Back to the theme of this book (if you haven't caught on just yet), it's all about tricking your f*ucking brain! If you change your thoughts to "watch this go in the hole" and you focus in only on holing the ball, you've taken a positive approach. This also has you taking a positive target and your thoughts are far away from mechanics, negativity, and doubt. All I can say is, once you practice this, you will be surprised how well it works. Again, don't make the first time you utilize this during a round of golf. You need to practice this first before you can bring it out on the course with you.

- Once you are on the green, the goal remains the same: every putt, I don't care how far, must be to make it. Now, I say this with caution, this does not mean hit it harder to make sure it gets there. If you're hitting the ball 10-15 feet past the hole consistently, the ball had no chance of going in the hole even if it hit it. The goal here is the "aim small, miss small" approach. The thought should be that you want to die it in the hole, not slam it in the hole. If you look at a 40-foot putt and think just get it to 3 feet and I'll be happy. Guess what? Your f*cking goal is now 3 feet. This is a common mistake for a lot of golfers. Of course, you would be thrilled if it ended up 3 feet from the hole. The issue is, if you don't achieve your goal, you're left with a 4-6-foot putt. I don't know about you, but those putts drive me crazy and they're tough on greens with a lot of imperfections. If you change your mindset to, "This is going to die in the hole," now if you miss, well, you just made a stress-free 2-putt. Your playing partner who chalked you up for a guaranteed 3-putt is now looking at his 8-foot putt for par a hell of a lot different, and all the pressure is now on him.

As with most concepts in golf, ignoring your brains desire to stress the f*ck out on every shot is much easier said than done. However, with practice and ultimately finding a method that works for you I think it's completely possible. The less time you spend worrying about your overall score and acting like every shot is a life or death situation, the more likely you are to remain consistent.

Shitty shots will still happen, and cart girls will still emerge from behind the trees just in time to see you hit your divot further than your ball. Sometimes the bad shots are just as important as the good ones. It's just the name of the game. The golfers who play every round like it's purely for practice even when the stakes are high, tend to be the ones walking away with the cash. Stop f*cking keeping score. Trust me.

Chapter 9: Go F*cking Practice

Like I have stated many times in this book, all these things came to me over a 15-year period and with a lot of f*cking practice. I don't want to understate the amount of practice it took. So, let me just paint a picture for you: imagine seeing some guy at the range swinging with one arm for three solid weeks. Yeah, that was me. I could care less what people thought, I was going to get better at golf, and I didn't care what it took. I was committed to getting better and loved putting in the time to get where I am today. I understand and appreciate that most people don't have the kind of patience and determination that was required to do this. My hope is that this book will allow the average golfer to start at the halfway point instead of at the starting line like I did.

I would equate this book, or any golf book for that matter, to a weight loss program. You can read the book, understand the concepts, and buy into the philosophy. Those things are pretty easy to do. Yet, if you never go to the gym and continue eating pizza and f*cking cheeseburgers, the program was a complete waste of your time. I have just given you the pathway to becoming a scratch golfer without spending thousands of dollars on professional swing lessons. Go f*cking practice.

It's cliché, but it really is a journey with a lot of ups and downs along the way. This game will test your patience like no other. If you stay true to the plan and prepare yourself that things may get worse before they get better, you will overcome the odds. This is the best f*cking game there is, and I wish I'd had the opportunity to play from a young age. But the best thing about this game, there is no such thing as starting too late. Now that you understand what you can do to reduce the variability in your approach to the game, you can really start enjoying it the way I do. Maybe you won't be club champ, but I can almost guarantee you will be playing better f*cking golf.

I'm always looking for feedback and constructive criticism, so please email me at info@bettergolfnow.com and let me know what you think of this book and if it's helped you improve your game. This is the 1000-foot view of how I transformed my golf game. I will dive deeper into each aspect of the game in a more focused approach in other books. Look out for Better F*cking Putting, Better F*cking Chipping, Better F*cking Irons, Better F*cking Tee Shots, and Better F*cking Golf Mentality.

Printed in Poland
by Amazon Fulfillment
Poland Sp. z o.o., Wrocław

64642070R00049